Izzy the Icky Iguana
Written and Illustrated
by Lori Kaiser

Another great book in the Xavier Series!

Published by
Carpe Diem Publishers
17401 Betty Blvd.
Canyon, TX 79015
281-635-2395

www.carpediempublishers.com

© Copyright, 2014 by Carpe Diem Publishers. All Rights Reserved. No portion of this book may be reproduced, stored in a retrieval system, or transmitted, in any form or by any means, electronic, mechanical, photocopying, recording, or otherwise without prior written permission from publisher.
Printed in the United States of America
ISBN 978-0-9883770-8-0

Dedicated to my son, Colton.
I love you so much and
I'm so proud of you.
Also dedicated to all moms
with little boys.

Apparently, bathing wasn't something he did well.

Then one day while Izzy chilled, sipping lemonade,

Who was this new iguana strolling into town? Big pink bow and long blonde hair, the prettiest around.

But the closer that he got,
the more that she could smell.

www.ingramcontent.com/pod-product-compliance
Lightning Source LLC
Chambersburg PA
CBHW050609300426
44112CB00013B/2140